WELCOME TO LEARN TO CODE WITH C

The C programming language was invented in the early 1970s, and since then has become one of the most popular and widely used general-purpose languages. It's used by a wide range of programmers, from amateurs working on simple projects at home, to industry professionals who write in C for a living. It's been used to program everything from the tiny microcontrollers used in watches and toasters up to huge software systems – most of Linux (and Raspbian itself) is written in it. It can give you control over the smallest details of how a processor operates, but is still simple to learn and read. This series is an introduction to programming in C for absolute beginners; you don't need any previous programming experience, and a Raspberry Pi running Raspbian is all you need to get started.

Simon Long

FIND US ONLINE raspberrypi.org/magpi   **GET IN TOUCH** magpi@raspberrypi.org

MagPi The

 Available on the **App Store**

 Google play

 CC BY NC SA

EDITORIAL
Publishing Director: **Russell Barnes**
Author: **Simon Long**
Sub Editors: **Lorna Lynch and Laura Clay**

DESIGN
Critical Media: **criticalmedia.co.uk**
Head of Design: **Dougal Matthews**
Designers: **Lee Allen, Mike Kay**

DISTRIBUTION
Seymour Distribution Ltd
2 East Poultry Ave, London
EC1A 9PT | **+44 (0)207 429 4000**

THE MAGPI SUBSCRIPTIONS
Select Publisher Services Ltd
PO Box 6337, Bournemouth
BH1 9EH | **+44 (0)1202 586 848**
magpi.cc/Subs1

The MagPi
ESSENTIALS

CONTENTS

[SIMON LONG]

Simon Long is a software engineer at Raspberry Pi, with a particular interest in user interface design. He first started writing C in the early 90s, and since then he's written software for a wide variety of electronic products, from mobile phones to medical equipment. Nowadays, he spends most of his time fiddling with the Raspbian desktop trying to make it better, and when he's not doing that, he's usually listening to 80s progressive rock and solving those really difficult crosswords without any black squares.

[CHAPTER ONE]
GETTING
STARTED

C is one of the most widely used programming
languages – learn how to use it to program the Pi!

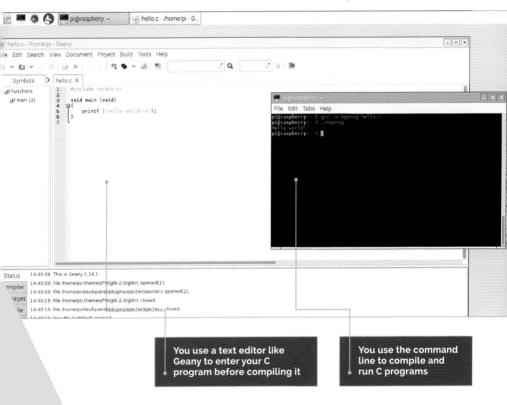

You use a text editor like Geany to enter your C program before compiling it

You use the command line to compile and run C programs

What's so great about C?

C is a very powerful language – there's not much you can't use it for – but it's fairly simple. The language itself only has 20 or so keywords, but there's a huge library of additional functions that you can call in when you need them. In this series, we're going to concentrate on learning about the keywords, with a few of the more useful library functions thrown in for good measure.

Many of the languages that you may have seen, such as Python, are what are called *interpreted languages*. This means that the code you write is run directly: each line of code is read in and interpreted as you run it. C is different: it's a *compiled language*. This means that the code you write, known as the *source code*, is never run directly. The source code is passed through a program called a *compiler*, which converts it into a machine-readable version called an *executable* or a *binary*; you then run the resulting executable.

This may seem complex, but it has a few big advantages. First, it means that you don't need to have a copy of C itself on every computer you want to run your program on; once compiled, the executable is stand-alone and self-contained. Second, the compilation process will find a lot of errors before you even run the program (but it won't usually find all of them). Most importantly, the compilation process means that the time-consuming translation of human-readable code into machine-readable instructions has already happened, which means that compiled code generally runs many times faster than interpreted code would.

Hello world – your first C program

With all that out of the way – which has hopefully made you think that C might be worth learning – let's have a look at the first program everyone writes in any language, the one that prints 'Hello World' on the screen. Incidentally, the tradition of writing a Hello World program was first introduced with the original documentation describing C itself. Just think: no C, no Hello World...

```c
#include <stdio.h>

void main (void)
{
    /* A print statement */
    printf ("Hello world!\n");
}
```

Hopefully not too frightening! Let's look at it line by line.

```c
#include <stdio.h>
```

This is known as a *hash-include*. As mentioned above, the C language has a large library of functions that can be included, and we need to use one of them in this program: the formatted print command **printf**. This is part of the standard input-output library, or **stdio** for short. So what this line does is to warn the compiler that the program needs the **stdio** library to be included as part of the compile process.

```
void main (void)
```

C is a function-based language; every program is made up of a number of functions.

Each function takes zero or more arguments, and returns a single value. A function definition consists of a specification of what the function returns (in this case, a **void**), a function name (in this case, **main**), and a list of arguments enclosed in round brackets (again, a **void**).

Every C program has to include a function called **main**; when you run the compiled program, the **main** function is the first thing that executes.

The word **void** is called a *type specifier*; a **void** is a special type which means 'no value required'. We'll look more at types in the next chapter.

So this line defines the **main** function for this program; it states that the **main** function takes no arguments, and returns no value.

The code which makes up the function itself is enclosed between the two curly brackets **{}** that follow the function definition.

```
/* A print statement */
```

First, we have a comment telling us what's going on. Comments in C start with the symbol **/***, and end with ***/** - anything between those two symbols is ignored by the compiler.

The code itself is just one line:

```
printf ("Hello world!\n");
```

This is a call to the **printf** ('print formatted') function from the **stdio** library. In this case, it takes a single argument, which is a text string enclosed within double quotes. As mentioned above, function arguments are enclosed in round brackets.

Note that the line ends with a semicolon. All statements in C must finish with a semicolon; this tells the compiler that this is the end of a statement. One of the most common beginner mistakes in C is to forget a semicolon somewhere!

What about the string itself? The **Hello World!** bit is straightforward enough, but what about that **\n** at the end? Remember this function is called 'print formatted'? Well, the **\n** is a bit of

[CHECK YOUR BRACKETS]

Unlike whitespace, punctuation is very important in C – make sure you don't use a curly bracket where a round one is needed, or vice versa.

Right You interact with both the C compiler and your compiled C programs from the command line; you can either do this in a terminal window in the desktop, or by booting your Pi straight to the command line

```
File  Edit  Tabs  Help
pi@raspberry:~ $ gcc -o myprog hello.c
pi@raspberry:~ $ ./myprog
Hello world!
pi@raspberry:~ $
```

formatting; it's the symbol for a newline character. So this line will print the string 'Hello World!', followed by a new line.

Compiling your program

Let's compile and run this. Raspbian includes a C compiler called gcc, so there's nothing to install; just start up Raspbian on your Pi and you're ready to go. Use your favourite text editor to create a file called **hello.c**, copy the program above into it, and save it. Then, from a terminal, go into the directory where you saved **hello.c** and enter:

```
gcc -o myprog hello.c
```

This calls the gcc C compiler with the option **-o myprog**, which tells it to create an executable output file called **myprog**, and to use **hello.c** as the input source code.

If you entered your C code correctly (did you make sure the semicolon was there?), this should take a second or so and then return you to the command line. There should now be a file in the current directory called **myprog** – try running it by typing:

```
./myprog
```

Et voila! You should now have...

```
Hello World!
```

...written in the terminal.

That's your first C program written, compiled, and run. In the next chapter, we'll start using C for something a bit more useful...

[RUNNING YOUR PROGRAM]

You need to tell Linux that the program you want to run is in the current directory, so don't forget the ./ before myprog, or it won't know where to look!

[CHAPTER TWO]
VARIABLES &
ARITHMETIC

Doing some real work in C: creating
variables and performing mathematical
operations on them

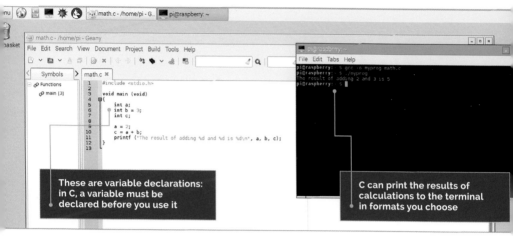

These are variable declarations: in C, a variable must be declared before you use it

C can print the results of calculations to the terminal in formats you choose

[MULTIPLE DECLARATIONS]

You can declare multiple variables of the same type in one line, separated by commas. For the example here, instead of three separate int declarations, you could type `int a, b = 3, c;` on one line.

In some languages, you can create variables as you go along and put whatever data you want into them. C isn't like that: to use a variable in C, you need to have created it first, and at the time you create it, you have to set what type of value it's going to store. By doing this, a block of memory of the correct size can be allocated by the compiler to hold the variable. This process of creating a variable is known as *declaration*.

Integers

There are several fundamental data types in C, but we'll start by looking at one of the most commonly used: the **int** type, used to store an integer value.

```c
#include <stdio.h>

void main (void)
{
    int a;
    int b = 3;
    int c;

    a = 2;
    c = a + b;
    printf ("The sum of adding %d and %d is %d\n", a, b, c);
}
```

The top three lines inside the main function here are declarations. They tell the compiler that we would like to use variables called **a**, **b** and **c** respectively, and that each one is of type **int**, i.e. an integer. In the second line, we see an example of an *initialisation* at the same time as a declaration: this stores an initial value of 3 in the variable **b**. Note that the values of **a** and **c** at this point are undefined; you might assume that a variable which hasn't had a value stored in it is always 0, but that isn't the case in C. Before reading the value from a variable or using it in a calculation, you must store a value in it; reading a variable before initialising it is a common error in C.

The next two lines do some actual work with the variables we have declared.

[ARITHMETIC SHORTHAND]

C allows shortcuts for some common operations; for example, instead of typing
a = a + 1,
you can just enter a++.
Or for
a = a * 3,
you can enter
a *= 3

```
a = 2;
```

This stores a value of 2 in the variable **a**, which will now have this value until it's changed. The reason **a** is called a variable is that it can vary: you can change its value as often as you like, but only to another integer. The value of a variable can change, but its type is fixed when it is declared.

```
c = a + b;
```

This line adds **a** to **b**, and stores the result in **c**.

```
printf ("The sum of adding %d and %d is %d\n", a, b, c);
```

This is another use of the formatted print function we saw in the previous chapter. Note the three **%d** symbols inside the string: these are *format specifiers*, and they are how you output numbers in C. When the **printf** function is executed, each **%d** is replaced by a decimal representation (d for decimal integer) of the variable in the corresponding position in the list after the string. So the first **%d** will be replaced by the value of **a**, the second with the value of **b**, and the third with the value of **c**.

Compile the program above and then run it. You should see this:

```
The sum of adding 2 and 3 is 5
```

...in the terminal.

Floating-point numbers

So we can add two integers together; what else can we do? One thing we might want to do is to use floating-point numbers: numbers with a decimal point. These have a different type, called **float**. Try changing the code above so instead of:

```
int a;
```

...you have:

```
float a;
```

This tells the compiler that **a** is now a floating-point value, rather than an integer. Compile and run your program. What happens?

Oops! That doesn't look right, does it? What has happened is that, while the maths is still all correct, the **printf** statement is now wrong; you're telling it to print **a**, which is a floating-point value, as a decimal integer. To fix that, change the first **%d** in the **printf** function to **%f**, which is the format specifier for a floating-point number, like this:

Below Don't forget to use %f instead of %d as the print specifier when changing the int values to float values in the example

[DECIMAL PLACES]

You can set the number of decimal places to display for a floating-point type-specifier in **printf** by putting a decimal point and the number of places between the % and the f – so %.3f will show a float value with three digits after the decimal point.

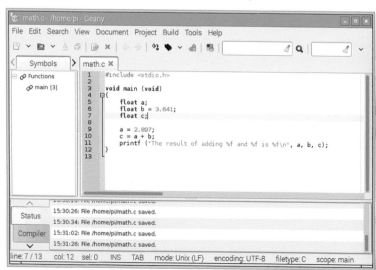

```
printf ("The sum of adding %f and %d is %d\n", a, b, c);
```

That should produce something a lot more sensible when you run it. This is an important lesson about C: it will do exactly what you tell it to, even if it makes no sense. You told it to show you a floating-point number as if it were a decimal integer, and the compiler assumed that was what you wanted, even though the result was nonsense.

When you're working with variables, always keep track of what values you're putting in what types, as it's easy to introduce errors by assuming a variable is of one type when it's actually another. One common error is to put the results of a calculation on floating-point values into an integer.

Try this: make **b** a float as well (not forgetting to change its format specifier in the **printf**), but leave **c** as an int, and set the two floats to values with decimal points, like this:

```
float a;
float b = 3.641;
int c;

a = 2.897;
c = a + b;
printf ("The sum of adding %f and %f is %d\n", a, b, c);
```

You'll see a result like:

```
The sum of adding 2.897000 to 3.641000 is 6
```

6? That's not right! But it's exactly what you've asked for. What the compiler did was to add the two floating-point values together, and got the answer 6.538, but you then told the compiler to put that into **c**, an integer variable. So the compiler just threw away everything after the decimal point! If you change **c** to a float, and change the final **%d** to **%f**, you'll find it gives the correct answer.

That gives you some idea about how C handles numbers, and how you can use it for arithmetic; in the next chapter, we'll look at how to use the results of calculations to make decisions.

[CHAPTER THREE]
CONDITIONS &
COMPARISONS

Branches and loops: controlling
the flow of your C program

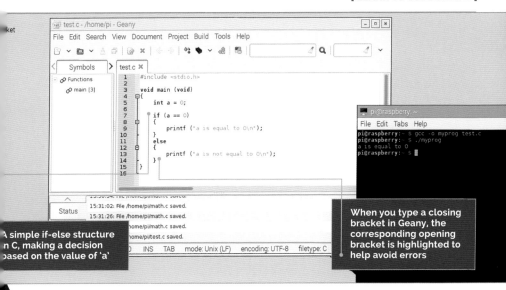

A simple if-else structure in C, making a decision based on the value of 'a'

When you type a closing bracket in Geany, the corresponding opening bracket is highlighted to help avoid errors

One of the fundamentals of any programming language is the ability to make conditional operations – to change the program's flow depending on the result of a test – and C allows you to do this. In this chapter, we'll look at how you test conditions within your C programs, and how you use the results to determine what happens next.

In C, the mechanism for controlling flow based on testing a condition is the *if-else* statement. Here's a simple example:

```c
#include <stdio.h>

void main (void)
{
    int a = 0;

    if (a == 0)
    {
        printf ("a is equal to 0\n");
    }
    else
    {
        printf ("a is not equal to 0\n");
    }
}
```

[CURLY BRACKETS]

Curly brackets are used to group together a set of statements which always execute together. If your loop or if statement only needs to execute one single statement, you can leave out the curly brackets after the test, but this can make the code's purpose less obvious to a human!

You can have multiple else statements in one test. Instead of one simple else for one alternative, use else if () with a new test for each alternative you want. We'll look more at this in the next chapter.

Here, the keyword **if** is followed by a test enclosed in round brackets, in this case **(a == 0)**. If the test evaluates as true, the operations enclosed by the curly brackets after the test are executed.

This example also shows the use of an else clause. At the end of the curly brackets around the operations which you want to execute if the test is true, there's an **else** followed by another set of curly brackets; these contain the operations you want to execute if the original test evaluated as false.

Try compiling the code above, and change the value with which **a** is initialised to make sure it does what you expect.

= or ==

That's all fine, but what's this **a == 0** all about? Surely if we want to know whether **a** is equal to 0, we just put **a = 0**. Why the two equals signs? Well, try replacing the double equals sign with a single equals and see what happens.

This is a very important aspect of C syntax, and a common source of bugs. The equals sign is used for two different things: one is to *assign* a value to a variable, whereas the other is to *test* whether a variable is equal to a value. A single equals sign (**=**) assigns a variable; a double equals sign (**==**) tests a variable.

So the statement...

```
if (a == 0)
```

...tests to see if **a** is equal to 0. If it is, then the test evaluates as true, and the code immediately after the **if** is executed.

But the statement...

```
if (a = 0)
```

...doesn't compare **a** against 0 at all: it just sets **a** to 0. So how does the compiler decide what to do next? In this case, it just looks at the value of what's in the brackets; you've set **a** to 0, so the value inside the brackets is 0.

In C, a value of 0 is equivalent to false, and a non-zero value is equivalent to true. So by replacing the double equals with a single equals, you've changed the value of **a**, and then you look to see if the

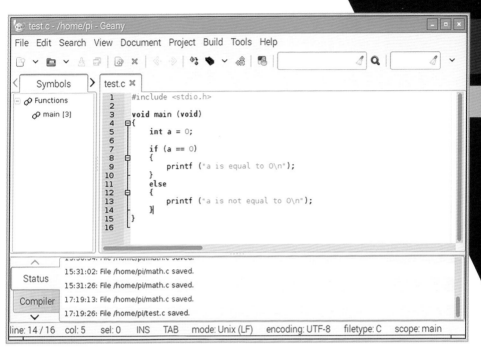

```
#include <stdio.h>

void main (void)
{
    int a = 0;

    if (a == 0)
    {
        printf ("a is equal to 0\n");
    }
    else
    {
        printf ("a is not equal to 0\n");
    }
}
```

Above Make sure that you use a double equals sign in the brackets after the **if**, not a single one!

value you've set **a** to is equivalent to true or false; neither of which were what you wanted to do! If a C program is behaving strangely, check very carefully that all your tests are actually tests and not assignments: this is a very easy mistake to make.

So **==** is the test to see if a value is equal to another one. There are other useful symbols that can be used in a test. The symbol **!=**, for example, means 'is not equal to'. The mathematical operators **>** and **<** are used to test for 'is greater than' and 'is less than' respectively, and they can also be combined with an equals sign to give **>=** and **<=**, the tests for 'is greater than or equal to' and 'is less than or equal to'.

You can combine tests with logical operators. The symbol **&&** is a Boolean AND (i.e. test whether both sides are true), and **||** is Boolean OR (i.e. test if either side is true). So, to execute code only if both **a** and **b** are 0, you would use **if (a == 0 && b == 0)**. To check if either **a** or **b** is 0, you use **if (a == 0 || b == 0)**.

Similarly, you can use the operator **!** as a Boolean NOT to invert the result of a test, so **if (!(a == 0))** is the same as **if (a != 0)**.

[INFINITE LOOPS]

Make sure your loops always finish! If the condition you test in a while loop never evaluates to false, your program will sit in the loop forever and never finish. If a program appears to be doing nothing when you run it, check your loop tests.

Looping

The if statement is useful for making a single decision, but what if you want to do something repeatedly until a test is true or false? We use a *while* loop for this, and here's an example:

```c
#include <stdio.h>

void main (void)
{
  int a = 0;

  while (a < 5)
  {
    printf ("a is equal to %d\n", a);
    a++;
  }
  printf ("a is equal to %d and I've finished\n", a);
}
```

This is very similar to an if statement, but the code in the curly brackets is executed repeatedly for as long as the test in the round brackets is true, not just once.

So in our example code, **a** is initialised to 0. We enter the while loop, and test to see if **a** is less than 5, which it is, so the code inside the curly brackets is executed. The value of **a** is printed out, then we have one of C's useful shortcuts to save too much typing…

a++ is the same as **a=a+1**; the double plus means 'add one to this variable'. Similarly, **a--** means 'subtract one from this variable'; these are very commonly used to count the times around a loop. The notation **a+=1** can also be used to add a value to a variable; this also works for other arithmetic operators, so **a*=3** multiplies **a** by 3, and so on.

In the while loop, each time the code in the curly brackets has been executed, the test in the round brackets is repeated; if it's still true, the loop code is repeated again. As soon as the test is false, execution continues with the line after the closing curly bracket.

Sometimes, we might want a loop which always runs at least once before a test is made. We do this with a small modification to the syntax to create a *do-while* loop:

```c
#include <stdio.h>

void main (void)
{
  int a = 0;

  do
  {
    printf ("a is equal to %d\n", a);
    a++;
  } while (a < 5);
  printf ("a is equal to %d and I've finished\n", a);
}
```

[MORE ABOUT SEMICOLONS]

Unlike the test in an if statement or a while loop, you need to put a semicolon after the test in a do-while loop. This indicates the end of the loop code; in a while loop, the loop code doesn't end until the last statement inside the curly brackets.

The keyword **do** now goes before the curly bracket, and the **while** and test go after the closing curly bracket. When this runs, the code in the loop always executes once before the test; you can test this by running both the loop examples above with **a** initialised to 5 rather than 0, and seeing how the behaviour differs.

```
pi@raspberrypi: ~                              _ □ ×
File  Edit  Tabs  Help
pi@raspberrypi:~ $ ./myprog
a is equal to 0
a is equal to 1
a is equal to 2
a is equal to 3
a is equal to 4
a is equal to 5 and I've finished
pi@raspberrypi:~ $
```

Left A loop executes the same code multiple times until the loop test is false

In the next chapter, we'll look at some more complex examples of looping and flow control.

CHAPTER FOUR
MORE ADVANCED
FLOW CONTROL

For loops and case statements – more advanced
ways of controlling the flow of a program

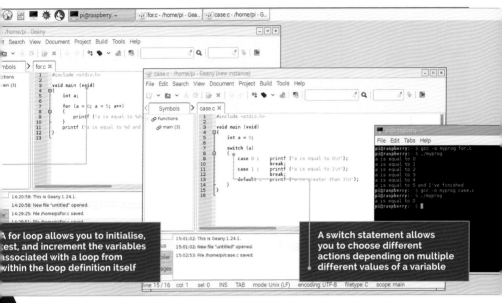

A for loop allows you to initialise, test, and increment the variables associated with a loop from within the loop definition itself

A switch statement allows you to choose different actions depending on multiple different values of a variable

The *if* statement and *while* loop described in the previous chapter are fairly simple control structures. In this chapter, we're going to look at a few more complex structures that can help to make your code shorter and reduce the amount of typing you need to do…

While the while loop we saw in the previous article is very useful, the *for* loop tends to be favoured by many programmers, as it puts all the logic controlling the loop in one place. Here's an example:

```c
#include <stdio.h>

void main (void)
{
  int a;

  for (a = 0; a < 5; a++)
  {
    printf ("a is equal to %d\n", a);
  }
  printf ("a is equal to %d and I've finished\n", a);
}
```

[MULTIPLE INITIALISATIONS]

You can initialise multiple variables in a for loop – just separate them by commas. So if you want to set two variables at the start of the loop, you can use `for (a = 0, b = 1;<test>; <increment>)`

This isn't all that different from a while loop, but all of the control for the loop lives in the round brackets after the **for** keyword. This contains three statements, separated by semicolons: in order, these are the *initial condition*, the *test*, and the *increment*.

a = 0 is the initial condition; the variable **a** is initialised to 0 at the start of the loop.

a < 5 is the test, just like in a while loop. This is checked on each iteration of the loop, and the loop code is only executed if the test evaluates to true; as soon as the test is false, execution continues after the curly bracket at the end of the loop code.

a++ is the increment; this is code which is executed at the end of each iteration of the loop, before the test is evaluated again. In this case, it adds 1 to **a**.

So when this for loop runs, what happens? First, **a** is set to 0. The test is then checked: is **a** (which is 0) less than 5? Yes it is, so the code inside the curly brackets is executed, and the value

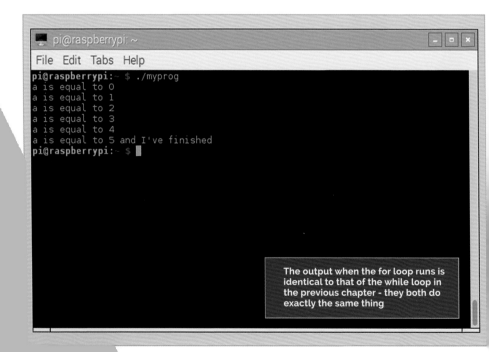

The output when the for loop runs is identical to that of the while loop in the previous chapter - they both do exactly the same thing

of **a** is printed. Finally, the increment is applied, meaning 1 is added to **a**.

The test is then repeated. If true, the loop code is executed again, and the increment is again applied; this repeats over and over until the test is false, at which point execution continues after the closing curly bracket.

In terms of what they do, for loops and while loops are pretty much identical; both wrap up a section of code you want to run more than once in some logic that controls how many times it runs. You can use whichever makes the most sense, or whichever looks tidiest to you!

Switch statements

One thing that you quite often want to do is to test a variable against several values, and do different things based on each of them. You can do this with a set of nested if statements:

```c
#include <stdio.h>

void main (void)
{
  int a = 0;

  if (a == 0)
  {
    printf ("a is equal to 0\n");
  }
  else if (a == 1)
  {
    printf ("a is equal to 1\n");
  }
  else
  {
    printf ("a is greater than 1\n");
  }
}
```

That does start to get pretty long-winded, though, so C provides a neater way of doing this, called a *switch* statement.

> **[MULTIPLE INCREMENTS]**
>
> As with multiple initialisations, you can have multiple increments in a for loop, also separated by commas – for (a = 0; b = 1; <test> ; a++, b *= 2). This is useful if there are two or more variables that change consistently while the loop runs.

```
#include <stdio.h>

void main (void)
{
  int a = 0;

  switch (a)
  {
    case 0 :    printf ("a is equal to 0\n");
                break;
    case 1 :    printf ("a is equal to 1\n");
                break;
    default :   printf ("a is greater than 1\n");
  }
}
```

This does exactly the same as the example above with multiple if statements, but is a lot shorter. So how does it work?

The opening line consists of the keyword **switch**, with the name of a variable in round brackets. This is the variable which will be tested against the various cases.

The body of the switch statement is a number of **case** statements. The variable **a** is compared against each case in turn; if it matches the value immediately after the word **case**, then the lines of code after the colon are executed.

The final case is just called **default** – every switch statement should include a default case as the final one in the list, and this is the code which is executed if none of the other cases match.

Notice that the last line in each case section is the word **break** – this is very important. The keyword **break** tells the compiler that you want to "break out" of the switch statement at this point; that is, to stop executing code inside the switch and to resume execution after the closing curly bracket. If you forget to include the break statements, every case after the one you wanted will execute as well as the one you wanted. Try it by compiling the code above and running it – you'll see the following in the terminal:

```
a is equal to 0
```

Now remove the two break statements, so the switch looks like:

```
switch (a)
{
    case 0 :    printf ("a is equal to 0\n");
    case 1 :    printf ("a is equal to 1\n");
    default :   printf ("a is greater than 1\n");
}
```

and run it again – you'll now see:

```
a is equal to 0
a is equal to 1
a is greater than 1
```

Not what you expected! This is another common bug in C code –
forgetting the break statements in your cases can result in very unexpected

Left Don't
forget the break
statements at the
end of each case
in your switch
statements!

[YOUR
FAVOURITE
LOOP...]

All three types
of loop in C –
while, do-while
and for – can
be used in
pretty much
any situation
where a loop
is needed;
choose
whichever
you like. Some
people prefer
to use one
type of loop
for everything;
others pick
and choose
whichever
looks tidiest
for each
circumstance.
There are no
wrong choices!

behaviour. But this can also be useful; programmers will sometimes structure a switch statement with code that they want to execute in multiple different cases, and deliberately leave out the break statements.

Leaving a loop early

The break statement has one other use; it can be used inside while and for loops to break out of them. Look at this example:

```c
#include <stdio.h>

void main (void)
{
  int a = 0;

  while (1)
  {
    printf ("a is equal to %d\n", a);
    a++;
    if (a == 5)
    {
      break;
    }
  }
  printf ("a is equal to %d and I've finished", a);
}
```

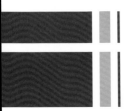

[CONTINUE]

The keyword **continue** can be used in a loop instead of **break**, but instead of breaking out of the loop, **continue** skips all the rest of the code in the current iteration, and returns to the test case at the start of the loop. Among other things, this can be useful to speed up your code.

So we have a while loop in which the test is just the value **1**; this is a non-zero value, and so is always true. If you enclose code inside curly brackets after a **while (1)** statement, the loop will never end; it will keep running forever. But in this case we have provided an alternative way to end the loop; we test the value of **a** inside the loop itself in an if statement, and if **a** is equal to 5, we call **break**. This causes the loop to end and execution to continue with the statement after the loop. A break statement like this can be useful to leave a loop early in the event of an error, for example.

That's about all you need to know about control flow in C; in the next chapter, we'll look at pointers, which are one of C's most useful and powerful features.

CHAPTER FIVE
POINTERS

Pointers – variables have addresses
as well as names…

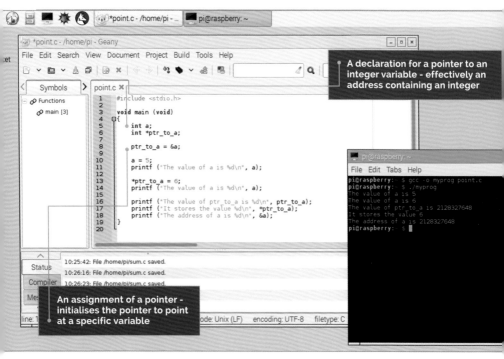

A declaration for a pointer to an integer variable - effectively an address containing an integer

```c
#include <stdio.h>

void main (void)
{
    int a;
    int *ptr_to_a;

    ptr_to_a = &a;

    a = 5;
    printf ("The value of a is %d\n", a);

    *ptr_to_a = 6;
    printf ("The value of a is %d\n", a);

    printf ("The value of ptr_to_a is %d\n", ptr_to_a);
    printf ("It stores the value %d\n", *ptr_to_a);
    printf ("The address of a is %d\n", &a);
}
```

An assignment of a pointer - initialises the pointer to point at a specific variable

---

[* AND &]

When I was first learning about pointers, I found it helpful to say out loud what a line of code was doing – an * is "what is pointed to by", and an & is "the address of". Once you've got those two ideas fixed in your head, you've pretty much understood pointers!

T he term *pointer* has struck fear into the heart of many a beginner C programmer, but once you've got your head around them, they are a very useful feature of the language. They aren't actually that complicated in reality, but it's easy to get confused when using them, so let's try to avoid that…

Remember when we looked at the declaration of variables? Declaring a variable – telling the compiler what type it is and what it's called – before you can use it is necessary in C, because the declaration enables the compiler to allocate a block of memory to store the variable. So for every variable you declare, there's a block of memory which is set aside by the compiler for that variable, and the compiler remembers which particular block of memory is used for each variable.

What is a pointer?

A pointer is just the address of a block of memory with a variable in it; that's all there is to it. So if you declare a variable and a pointer to that variable, you can access the value in that block of memory in two ways; either with the variable name, or with the pointer.

Let's look at a simple example:

```c
#include <stdio.h>

void main (void)
{
  int a;
  int *ptr_to_a;

  ptr_to_a = &a;

  a = 5;
  printf ("The value of a is %d\n", a);

  *ptr_to_a = 6;
  printf ("The value of a is %d\n", a);

  printf ("The value of ptr_to_a is %d\n", ptr_to_a);
  printf ("It stores the value %d\n", *ptr_to_a);
  printf ("The address of a is %d\n", &a);
}
```

Taking it line by line, the first line is one we're already familiar with: we declare an integer variable called **a**. But what's this?

```c
int *ptr_to_a;
```

This looks like it's declaring another integer variable, doesn't it? But look more carefully; the asterisk (*****) at the start of the variable name indicates that this is not declaring an integer variable, but a *pointer to* an integer variable.

So we now have an integer variable called **a**, and we have a pointer to an integer variable, called **ptr_to_a**. But neither of these actually have a value in them yet: they are both uninitialised. It's all very well calling the pointer **ptr_to_a**, but it has no idea what (or where) **a** is, so we'll fix that with the next line.

```c
ptr_to_a = &a;
```

Pointers are one of the ways C allows (or in some cases forces) you to think about what the actual hardware of your computer is doing - a good understanding of pointers gives you a good understanding of how the compiler handles memory.

This is the important bit! In C, the symbol **&** before a variable name means *address of the variable*, so **&a** means "the address in memory of the variable **a**". And as we said above, a pointer is the address of a variable. So this line initialises **ptr_to_a** to be the address of **a**; **ptr_to_a** is now a valid pointer to the variable **a**, so we can now use it.

The next two lines are familiar; we set **a** to be 5, and just to check that worked, we print its value. So let's try doing the same thing, but with the pointer.

```
*ptr_to_a = 6;
```

That asterisk again, but used in a slightly different way from before. When declaring a variable, putting an asterisk before its name indicates that the variable is a pointer. But once the pointer exists, putting an asterisk in front of its name means *the variable pointed to by this pointer*; this is known as *dereferencing* the pointer. So this line tells the compiler to set the variable pointed to by the pointer **ptr_to_a** to 6. We know that the variable pointed to by **ptr_to_a** is **a**; we set that up a couple of lines back, and so this line is just another way of setting **a** to 6; indeed, if we print the value of **a**, we find it has changed to 6.

The next lines will hopefully help you get the relationship between pointers, variables, and addresses clear in your mind.

```
printf ("The value of ptr_to_a is %d\n", ptr_to_a);
```

In this line, we're printing the value of **ptr_to_a**; not the value it's pointing at, but the value of the pointer itself. This prints a very large number, as it's the address in memory where **a** can be found.

```
printf ("It stores the value %d\n", *ptr_to_a);
```

In this line, we're printing the value pointed to by **ptr_to_a**; note the asterisk before the name. This prints the value of **a**.

```
printf ("The address of a is %d\n", &a);
```

Finally, in this line we're printing the address of **a** itself; note the **&** sign before the name. Again, this prints a very large number, the same as the value of **ptr_to_a** we printed above.

The crucial thing to remember when working with pointers is this: you can't just declare a pointer, as you need to also declare and associate the variable you want it to point to. When a pointer is created, it points at a random location in memory; if you try and write something to it, you can cause all sorts of errors up to and including crashing the computer completely! Always make sure your pointers are pointing at something before doing anything with them.

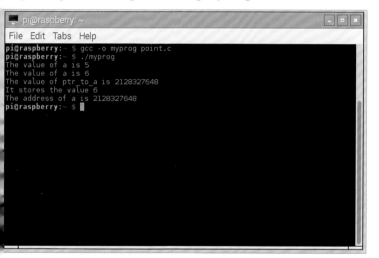

Above The example code shows clearly the relationship between a pointer and the actual address in memory of a variable - note that the address of **a** is identical to the value of the pointer. (The actual address will probably be different when you run the code, but the pointer and the address will still have the same value.)

Void pointers and casting

You can also define a pointer without saying what type of variable it's pointing to; this is a *void pointer*, written as **void ***. If you think about it, this makes sense; a pointer is just an address in memory, so we don't necessarily need to know what is at that memory. To use a void pointer, you need to *cast* it; you tell the compiler what sort of pointer to treat it as, and what sort of variable is in memory at that location. Here's an example:

[ALWAYS HAVE SOMETHING TO POINT TO!]

It's worth stressing this again: a pointer is not a piece of memory, it's just an address of memory. If you want to do anything with a pointer, you need to declare something for it to point to as well as the pointer itself.

```
#include <stdio.h>

void main (void)
{
  int intval = 255958283;
  void *vptr = &intval;

  printf ("The value at vptr as an int is %d\n", *((int *) vptr));
  printf ("The value at vptr as a char is %d\n", *((char *) vptr));
}
```

We initialise the void pointer **vptr** to point to an integer variable called **intval**.

In the first **printf** statement, we insert **(int *)** in front of **vptr** before we dereference it using *****. This casts **vptr** to an integer pointer, and so the value of **intval** is printed as an integer.

In the second **printf** statement, we insert **(char *)** in front of **vptr** before we dereference it. This casts **vptr** to a char pointer, and so what's printed is the value of the char which makes up the first byte of **intval**.

[INCREMENTING POINTERS]

You can use ++ and -- on pointers, but you need to be careful. (*a)++ increments the value pointed to by a, but *(a++) increments the pointer itself rather than the value it points at - this will move a to point at the memory address immediately after a.

What do you use pointers for?

That's really all there is to pointers, other than to ask why bother? We can already access a variable with its name, so why do we need to have some complicated alternative way of getting to the contents of a variable?

There are several ways in which pointers are useful, which we will explore in more detail in later chapters. But a few of the important ones are:

> **function calls** – in the next chapter we will look at how to split up C code into functions; pointers are very useful for allowing a function to return multiple values.
> **string handling** – in C, a string is a continuous block of memory with a letter stored in each byte; pointers make it possible to perform efficient operations on strings.
> **arrays** – C allows array variables, lists of values of the same type, which like strings are stored in a continuous block of memory; pointers make accessing arrays easier and more efficient.

CHAPTER SIX]
FUNCTIONS

Functions - how to split your code
up into easy bite-sized chunks…

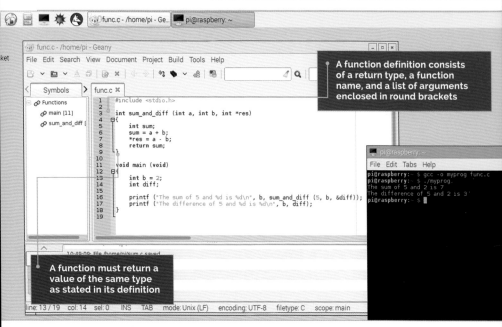

A function definition consists of a return type, a function name, and a list of arguments enclosed in round brackets

A function must return a value of the same type as stated in its definition

[ARGUMENTS]

A function can have any number of **arguments**, from zero up to hundreds. If you don't need any arguments, you list the arguments as (**void**) in the function definition (just like in the **main** function); when you call the function, just put a pair of empty round brackets () after the function name.

p until now, all the examples we've looked at have had one single function, **main**, with all the code in it. This is perfectly valid for small, simple programs, but it's not really practical once you get more than a few tens of lines, and it's a waste of space if you need to do the same thing more than once. Splitting code up into separate functions makes it more readable and enables easy reuse. We've already seen functions used; the **main** function is a standard C function, albeit with a special name. We've also seen the **printf** function called by our examples. So how do we create and use a function of our own? Here's an example:

```c
#include <stdio.h>

int sum (int a, int b)
{
    int res;
    res = a + b;
    return res;
}
```

```
void main (void)
{
  int y = 2;
  int z = sum (5, y);

  printf ("The sum of 5 and %d is %d\n", y, z);
}
```

This includes both the **main** function and a second function called **sum**. In both cases, the structure of the function is the same: a line defining the value returned by the function, the function name, and the function arguments, followed by a block of code enclosed within curly brackets, which is what the function actually does.

What's in a function?

Let's look at the **sum** function:

```
int sum (int a, int b)
```

The definition of a function has three parts. The first part is the type of the value returned by the function: in this case, an **int**. The second part is the name of the function: in this case, **sum**. Finally, within round brackets are the arguments to the function, separated by commas, and each is given with its type: in this case, two integer arguments, **a** and **b**.
  The rest of the function is between the curly brackets.

```
int res;
```

This declares a *local variable* for the function, an integer called **res**. This is a variable which can only be used locally, within the function itself. Variables declared within a function definition can only be used within that function; if you try and read or write **res** within the main function, you'll get an error. (You could declare another **int** called **res** within the main function, but this would be a different variable called **res** from the one within the **sum** function, and would get very confusing, so it's not recommended!)

[VARIABLE SCOPE]

If you declare a variable within a function, it's only usable within that function, not within any functions which call the function, or within functions called by the function. This is known as the *scope* of a variable: the parts of the code in which it's valid.

```
res = a + b;
```

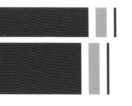

This should be obvious! Note that **a** and **b** are the two defined arguments of the function. When a function is called, a local copy of the arguments is made and used within the function. If you change the values of **a** or **b** within the function (which is a perfectly valid thing to do), that only affects the value of **a** and **b** within this function; it doesn't change the values that the arguments had in the function from which it was called.

```
return res;
```

Finally, we need to return the result. The function was defined to return an integer, so it must call the **return** statement with an integer value to be returned to the calling function.

A function doesn't have to return a value; if the return type is set to **void**, it returns nothing. There's no need for a **return** statement in a function with a **void** return type; the function will return when it reaches the last line; however, if you want to return early (in the event of an error, for example), you just call **return** with no value after it.

Calling a function

Let's look at how we call the function from **main**:

```
int z = sum (5, y);
```

[RETURNING VALUES]

A function can return a single value, or no value at all. If you define the function as returning **void**, there's no need to use a **return** statement in it, but you'll get an error if you don't include a **return** of the correct type in a non-void function.

Above The main function prints out the values returned by the sum function

The **sum** function returns an integer, so we set an integer variable equal to it. The arguments we supply to the function are inside round brackets, and in the same order as in the function definition; so in this case, **a** is 5, and **b** is the value of **y**.

Can you return more than one result from a function? You can only return one value, but you can also use pointers to pass multiple items of data back to the calling function. Consider this example:

```c
#include <stdio.h>

int sum_and_diff (int a, int b, int *res)
{
  int sum;
  sum = a + b;
  *res = a - b;
  return sum;
}

void main (void)
{
  int b = 2;
  int diff;

  printf ("The sum of 5 and %d is %d\n", b,
    sum_and_diff (5, b, &diff));
  printf ("The difference of 5 and %d is %d\n", b, diff);
}
```

We've modified the **sum** function to calculate both the sum and the difference of the arguments. The sum is returned as before, but we're also passing the difference back using a pointer. Remember that the arguments to a function are local variables; even if you change one in the function, it has no effect on the value passed by the calling function. This is why pointers are useful; by passing a pointer, the function doesn't change the value of the pointer itself, but it can change the value in the variable to which it's pointing.

So we call the function with the same two arguments as before, but

Right By using a pointer as one argument, the `sum_and_diff` function can return both the sum and difference of the arguments

we add a third one, a pointer to the variable where we want to write the difference calculated by the function. In the function, we have this line:

```
*res = a – b;
```

The difference is written to the variable to which **res** is a pointer. In the main function, we call the **sum_and_diff** function like this:

```
sum_and_diff (5, b, &diff)
```

We provide the address of the integer **diff** as the pointer argument to the **sum_and_diff** function; when the difference is calculated, it's written into the variable **diff** in the main function.

Order matters

One thing to bear in mind when defining functions is that the compiler reads files from top to bottom, and you need to tell it about a function before you can use it. In the examples above, this is automatic, as the definition of the **sum** and **sum_and_diff** functions is before the first call to them in **main**.

```
func.c - /home/pi - Geany
File  Edit  Search  View  Document  Project  Build  Tools  Help

Symbols      func.c ×
Functions      1    #include <stdio.h>
  main [11]    2
  sum_and_diff 3    int sum_and_diff (int a, int b, int *res)
               4    {
               5        int sum;
               6        sum = a + b;
               7        *res = a - b;
               8        return sum;
               9    }
              10
              11    void main (void)
              12    {
              13        int b = 2;
              14        int diff;
              15
              16        printf ("The sum of 5 and %d is %d\n", b, sum_and_diff (5, b, &diff));
              17        printf ("The difference of 5 and %d is %d\n", b, diff);
              18    }
              19

Status     10:49:09: File /home/pi/sum.c saved.
           10:49:16: File /home/pi/point.c saved.
Compiler   10:54:56: File /home/pi/point.c saved.
Messages   10:55:04: File /home/pi/func.c saved.
           10:55:16: File /home/pi/func.c saved.

line: 13 / 19   col: 14   sel: 0   INS   TAB   mode: Unix (LF)   encoding: UTF-8   filetype: C   scope: main
```

Left You can use a function call wherever a variable of the same type as the value returned by the function could be used - in the code here, a call to `sum_and_diff` replaces an integer value in the arguments to `printf`.

But in larger files, when multiple functions call multiple other functions, this gets complicated; it's not always easy to make sure the function definitions are all in the right order. To avoid this, C allows you to *declare* functions before they are used.

A function declaration is just the definition of the function, minus the function code within the curly brackets. So for the **sum_and_diff** function, the declaration would be:

```
int sum_and_diff (int a, int b, int *res);
```

Note the semicolon at the end! Function declarations are included at the top of the file; when the compiler finds a function declaration, it knows that at some point a function with this name, arguments, and return type will be defined, so it then knows how to handle a call to it, even if it hasn't yet seen the definition itself.

CHAPTER SEVEN
ARRAYS &
STRINGS

How to handle arrays (lists of values)
and strings (lists of letters) in C

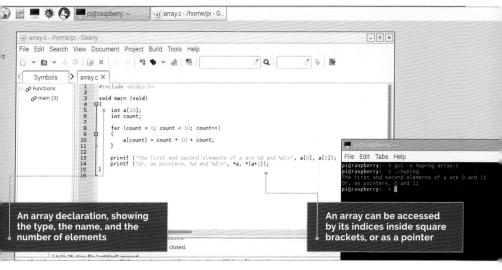

An array declaration, showing the type, the name, and the number of elements

An array can be accessed by its indices inside square brackets, or as a pointer

he variables we have looked at so far are all single numeric values. In this chapter, we're going to look at how C handles lists of values, and that leads into using lists of letters to store and manipulate text strings.

An *array* is a single variable which stores multiple different values of the same type; the individual values are accessed by *indexing* the array. An array can have one or more *dimensions*; a one-dimensional array is a single list of values, while a two-dimensional array is a list of lists of values, and so on.

An array is declared in C by putting the size of each dimension in square brackets after the variable name. So

```
int a[10];
```

is a list of 10 integers, while

```
int b[5][6];
```

is a list of 5 lists, each of which contains 6 integers.

When accessing the elements inside an array, the array index - the number inside the bracket - starts at 0. So the 10 integers contained within array **a** above are referred to as **a[0]**, **a[1]**, **a[2]** and so on up to **a[9]**. The compiler will quite happily allow you to read or write **a[10]**, **a[11]** or indeed **a[**any number you like**]**, but these are all outside the memory which was allocated when the array was declared, so writing to them is a really bad idea!

[KEEP INSIDE
YOUR ARRAY]

One of the
nastiest
sources of
crashes and
bugs in C is
creating an
array and then
writing past
the end of it.
The compiler
won't stop
you writing
to memory
off the end of
an array, and
doing so can
have serious
consequences.
Always make
sure your
array indices
fit inside
your array.

Arrays and pointers

This brings us on to the relationship between pointers and arrays.
The name of an array is effectively a pointer to the first element of the
array. Remember that a pointer is the address of a variable in memory?
Well, an array is a contiguous block of memory which contains all the
elements of the array in order, so you can use a pointer to access it. (In
fact, even if you use values in square brackets to access it, the compiler
treats those as a pointer anyway.) Here's an example:

```c
#include <stdio.h>

void main (void)
{
   int a[10];
   int count;

   for (count = 0; count < 10; count++)
   {
      a[count] = count * 10 + count;
   }

   printf ("The first and second elements of a are %d and %d\n",
      a[0], a[1]);
   printf ("Or, as pointers, %d and %d\n", *a, *(a+1));
}
```

This fills the 10 values of **a** with the numbers 0, 11, 22, 33, and
so on, and then reads **a[0]** and **a[1]**. It then reads the same values
using **a** as a pointer, and you can see if you run the code that they
are identical.

With a two-dimensional array or greater, you need to consider
how the compiler arranges the dimensions in memory; it does so by
grouping the elements at the rightmost index of the array together.
With the array **b[5][6]** above, **b** itself points at **b[0][0]**. **b+1** points
at **b[0][1]**; **b+5** points at **b[0][5]**; and **b+6** points at **b[1][0]**.

You can initialise an array at the same time as you declare it by
putting the values in curly brackets, so:

```
int a[10] = { 0, 11, 22, 33, 44, 55, 66, 77, 88, 99 };
```

But note that this only works when the array is first declared; once it exists, you can't use this shortcut and will need to iterate through the array indices, setting each value in turn.

Above Array elements are stored sequentially in memory, with the array name a pointer to the first element. Multi-dimensional array elements are stored with the elements with neighbouring values, in the rightmost index next to each other

Strings

In C, a string is just another array; it's an array of single characters. A character is a specific type in C, called **char**; this holds a single byte, which is enough to hold an alphanumeric character. So a string with ten bytes would be:

```
char mystring[10];
```

Or, to initialise it at the same time:

```
char mystring[10] = "thestring";
```

One important thing to remember is that a string in C must always end with a byte set to zero, and that the memory required to hold this final zero (called the *string terminator*) must be allocated when you declare the string. So **mystring**, which is declared as an array of 10 **char**s, can only actually hold text of 9 or fewer letters.

[NAMES ARE POINTERS]

Remember that the name of an array or a string is just a pointer to the first element of the array or string in question, and can be used in the same way as any other pointer; it can be incremented and decremented, or dereferenced to find the value to which it points.

Below Strings are stored as an array of single characters, with the element after the last character set to zero

You can use the index in square brackets to access individual characters in a string, or you can use a pointer. Here's an example of using pointers to join two strings together:

```c
#include <stdio.h>

void main (void)
{
  char str1[10] = "first";
  char str2[10] = "second";
  char str3[20];

  char *src, *dst;

  src = str1;
  dst = str3;
  while (*src != 0)
  {
    *dst = *src;
    src++;
    dst++;
  }
  src = str2;
  while (*src != 0)
  {
    *dst = *src;
    src++;
    dst++;
  }
  *dst = 0;

  printf ("%s + %s = %s\n", str1, str2, str3);
}
```

[TERMINATING STRINGS]

Always remember that the memory you allocate for a string needs to be long enough to hold all the characters, plus one extra to store the terminating zero. If you're manipulating strings yourself with pointers, make sure you remember to write the zero at the end of any string you create.

First, we create two strings – **str1** is "first" and **str2** is "second" – and we allocate an empty string, **str3**, to put the result in.

We then create a pair of **char** pointers, and point **src** at the start of **str1** (the "f" of "first") and **dst** at the start of the empty

str3. We then loop, copying what's at **src** to **dst**, and then moving both pointers forward by one, until we find the zero that terminates **str1**.

We then point **src** at **str2**, and do the same thing again, until we find the zero at the end of **str2**. Finally, we write a zero to the end of **str3** to terminate it. Note the new format specifier used to print strings; **%s** is used to print a string, and will display every character from the pointer supplied as an argument, up to the first terminating zero it finds. (If you want to print a single character, you can use the format specifier **%c**.)

Writing to strings

Because the name of a string variable is only a pointer to the first character of the string, you can't just use an equals sign to set the value of a complete string. You can initialise a string variable at the time you declare it, as above, but what if you want to set or change it later?

There are a few ways to do this, but the most useful is the **sprintf** function; this is a version of the **printf** function we have already seen, which writes arbitrary text to string variables. The only difference is that the first argument it takes is the name of a string variable, and it writes to that instead of to the terminal:

```c
#include <stdio.h>

void main (void)
{
    int val = 12;
    char string[50];

    sprintf (string, "The value of val is %d\n", val);
    printf ("%s", string);
}
```

The **sprintf** function will automatically add the terminating zero at the end of any string you create with it.

In the next chapter, we'll look at some of the functions provided in C's string handling library to make working with strings easier.

CHAPTER EIGHT
THE STRING
LIBRARY

Using the C string library to simplify
common operations on strings

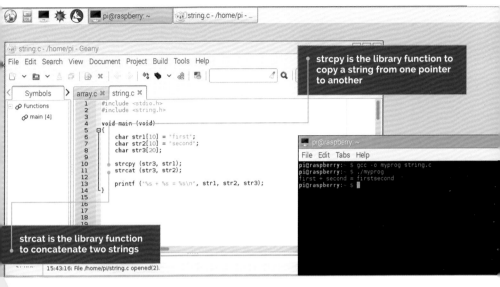

strcpy is the library function to copy a string from one pointer to another

strcat is the library function to concatenate two strings

n the previous chapter, we saw how to access strings using pointers. This works perfectly well, and gives you a good understanding of how pointers work, but it's a bit long-winded. Fortunately, C provides a library of useful string functions, which save a lot of typing!

In the last chapter, we saw how to join two strings together using pointers. We're going to do the same thing using the string handling library. Here's the code rewritten using string library functions:

```c
#include <stdio.h>
#include <string.h>

void main (void)
{
  char str1[10] = "first";
  char str2[10] = "second";
  char str3[20];

  strcpy (str3, str1);
  strcat (str3, str2);

  printf ("%s + %s = %s\n", str1, str2, str3);
}
```

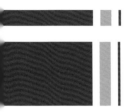

That's a lot shorter! Note the **#include <string.h>** at the start, which tells the compiler we want to use functions from the string library.

This shows us two string functions. **strcpy** ('string copy') copies the string at the second argument to the start of string at the first argument. **strcat** ('string concatenate') does the same thing, but instead of copying to the start of the first argument, it finds the terminating zero of the first argument and starts copying to its location, thus joining the two strings together.

Comparing strings

Another common requirement is to be able to compare two strings to see if they are the same. As we've already seen, we can compare numeric values with the **==** operator, but this doesn't work with strings. Remember that the name of a string is really just a pointer to a location in memory containing the string, so using **==** to compare two strings will only tell you if they're at the same place in memory, not if two strings at different locations are the same.

You can use **==** to compare two **char** variables, and a string is an array of **char**s, so it's possible to write a simple piece of code that compares each character in a string in turn:

```
#include <stdio.h>

void main (void)
{
  char str1[10] = "first";
  char str2[10] = "fire";
  char *ptr1 = str1, *ptr2 = str2;

  while (*ptr1 != 0 && *ptr2 != 0)
  {
    if (*ptr1 != *ptr2)
    {
        break;
    }
    ptr1++;
    ptr2++;
  }
```

```c
if (*ptr1 == 0 && *ptr2 == 0)
{
    printf ("The two strings are identical.\n");
}
else
{
    printf ("The two strings are different.\n");
}
```

But that's a bit tedious to write out every time, so the string library has done this for you with the function **strcmp** (for 'string compare'). Here's how you use it:

```c
#include <stdio.h>
#include <string.h>

void main (void)
{
    char str1[10] = "first";
    char str2[10] = "fire";
    if (strcmp (str1, str2) == 0)
    {
        printf ("The two strings are identical.\n");
    }
    else
    {
        printf ("The two strings are different.\n");
    }
}
```

[DON'T OVERWRITE]

It looks like it ought to be possible to use **strcpy** and **strcat** to copy part of a string over itself - **strcpy (a + 1, a)**, for example. Don't try it! The source and destination buffers for **strcpy** and **strcat** must be completely separate areas of memory; if not, their behaviour is unpredictable.

strcmp takes two strings as arguments, and returns a 0 if they're the same; it returns a non-zero value if not.

What about if you just want to compare the first few characters of a string, not the whole string? There's a library function for that, too: **strncmp** (for 'string numbered compare').

The MagPi
ESSENTIALS

[IGNORING CASE]

There are versions of **strcmp** and **strncmp** which ignore the case of the letters in the strings being compared; they're called **strcasecmp** and **strncasecmp**, respectively. They take the same arguments and return the same values.

This works in exactly the same way as **strcmp**, but it takes a third argument, an integer giving the number of characters to compare. So **strncmp ("first", "fire", 4)** would return a non-zero value, while **strncmp ("first", "fire", 3)** would return a 0.

Reading values from a string

We saw in the previous chapter that we can use **sprintf** to write variables into a string; what about being able to read variables back out of a string? The function **sscanf** ('string scan formatted') does that for you. Here's how it works:

```c
#include <stdio.h>

void main (void)
{
  int val;
  char string[10] = "250";

  sscanf (string, "%d", &val);
  printf ("The value in the string is %d\n", val);
}
```

sscanf uses exactly the same format specifiers as **printf**. One important difference, though, is that the arguments to **sscanf** must all be pointers to variables, rather than variables themselves. As always, a function can never change the values of variables provided as arguments, but it can write to their destinations if they are pointers.

You can check whether **sscanf** was able to match the format specifiers with the string provided by looking at the value it returns; **sscanf** returns the number of values it successfully read. So for example, if a format specifier of **%d** is provided but the string supplied doesn't start with a decimal number, **sscanf** will write nothing to the supplied pointer and will return 0; if the string supplied does start with a decimal number, **sscanf** will return 1.

Left The `sscanf`
library function is
used here with the
`%d` format specifier
to read the
decimal value 250
out of a string

The format string supplied to **sscanf** can contain multiple format specifiers and even other text:

```c
#include <stdio.h>

void main (void)
{

  int val;
  char result[10];
  char string[25] = "The first number is 1";

  if (sscanf (string, "The %s number is %d", result, &val) == 2)
  {
    printf ("String : %s Value : %d\n", result, val);
  }
  else
  {
    printf ("I couldn't find two values in that string.\n");
  }
```

[SSCANF STRINGS]

The **%s** format specifier matches a set of non-whitespace characters in **sscanf**; it will extract the first set of letters, numbers or punctuation up to the first space, tab or newline it finds in the string being scanned. A space in the format string matches one or more whitespace characters, not just a single space.

Note that, slightly inconsistently, the **%s** format specifier denotes a pointer to a string in both **printf** and **sscanf**, while the **%d** specifier denotes a *variable* in **printf** but a *pointer* in **sscanf**.

One thing to note about **sscanf** is that it's in the standard I/O library, not the string handling library, so you don't need **#include string.h>** to use it.

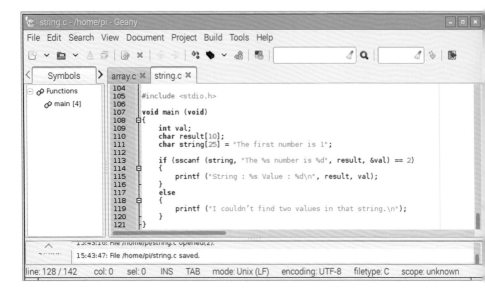

Above sscanf reads numeric values and words out of a formatted string, allowing you to parse text from elsewhere.

Remember that all the arguments to sscanf must be pointers

How long is a (piece of) string?

One final useful string handling function is **strlen** (for 'string length'); as the name suggests, this tells you how many characters there are in a string, counting from the start to the terminating zero character.

```c
#include <stdio.h>
#include <string.h>

void main (void)
{
  char str1[10] = "first";

  printf ("The length of the string '%s' is %d\n", str1,
    strlen (str1));
}
```

All the operations we've looked at here are possible by manually manipulating pointers; the string library just makes them easier and will make your code shorter. If you find yourself moving pointers around strings in a program, always check the string library to make sure you're not reinventing the wheel!

[CHAPTER **NINE**]
USER **INPUT**

Reading and interpreting
input from the user

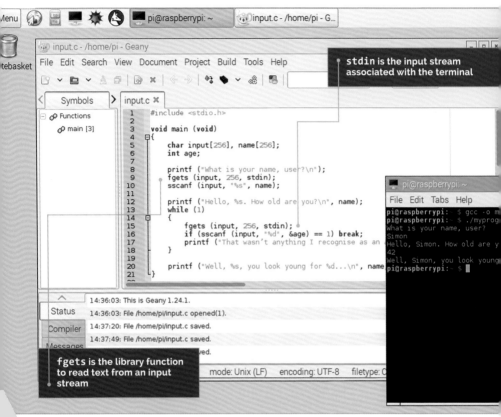

stdin is the input stream associated with the terminal

fgets is the library function to read text from an input stream

I n the previous chapter, we looked at how to print program output to the terminal, but in order to interact with the user, this needs to be a two-way process. This chapter looks at how we can read and interpret input that the user enters in the terminal.

We've seen the **printf** function used a lot in previous chapters; it's the standard way of writing formatted text output from a program to the *console*, the command line from which you run the program. But what if you want to get input from the user? How do we read what the user types into the console?

In the last chapters, we looked at the **sscanf** function which reads values from a string. There's an equivalent function called **scanf**, which reads values directly from the console, as in the following example:

```
#include <stdio.h>

void main (void)

  char input[256];
  int age;

  printf ("What is your name, user?\n");
  scanf ("%s", input);

  printf ("Hello, %s. How old are you?\n", input);
  scanf ("%d", &age);

  printf ("Well, %s, you look young for %d...\n", input, age);
```

scanf works exactly like **sscanf**, but has one fewer argument, as it reads from the console rather than from a string.

However, it's not really the best way of getting console input; it only really works if you have a user who types in exactly what you expect. Unfortunately, users have a nasty tendency to type in things you aren't expecting, and **scanf** doesn't cope well with this. For example, in the code above, if the user types in 257 characters when asked for their name, they will overflow the space allocated for the input string, and bad things may happen…

A better way

A better approach is to read each line the user enters into a buffer string, and then use **sscanf** to read values from that string. The C library function **fgets** is useful for this. Have a look at this example:

```c
#include <stdio.h>

void main (void)
{
    char input[256], name[256];
    int age;

    printf ("What is your name, user?\n");
    fgets (input, 256, stdin);
    sscanf (input, "%s", name);

    printf ("Hello, %s. How old are you?\n", name);
    while (1)
    {
        fgets (input, 256, stdin);
        if (sscanf (input, "%d", &age) == 1) break;
        printf ("I don't recognise that as an age - try again!\n")
    }

    printf ("Well, %s, you look young for %d...\n", name, age)
}
```

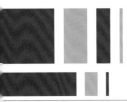

fgets takes three arguments. The first is the buffer into which it should store the input. The second is the maximum number of bytes it will write into that buffer; this is useful to prevent the overflow situation mentioned above. Finally, it takes an argument telling it where to read from; in this case, this is set to **stdin** (short for 'standard input'), which tells it to read from the console.

So each time we ask the user for input, we use **fgets** to read up to 256 characters of whatever they type (up to the point at which they press the enter key), and we then use **sscanf** to interpret it. Additionally, when asking for the user's age, we use the value returned by **sscanf**

described in the previous chapter) to check that the user has entered what you expect, and loop until they give a valid answer. You can use this method to interpret pretty much anything a user types, and to safely handle all the cases where they type something unexpected!

Reading parameters

There's another way to get input to your program, which is to supply it as a parameter when you start the program from the command line. At this point, I have to admit to not having been entirely honest for the last 8 chapters… I've always shown the definition of the **main** function as

```
void main (void)
```

This works, as you've seen, but it isn't strictly correct. The strict definition of main looks like this:

```
int main (int argc, char *argv[])
```

But let's be honest: if I'd shown you that in chapter 1, you'd have run a mile, wouldn't you? So what does it all mean?

First off, we can see that **main** returns an integer; this is a success or failure code which some operating systems can use for processing in a shell script or the like. Traditionally, if a program succeeds, **main** returns 0, and if it fails, it returns a non-zero error code. For programs that run on their own, you really don't need to worry about it!

What's more useful are the other two arguments. **argc** is an integer, and this is the number of parameters which were provided on the command line when the program was started. Strangely, the number includes the program name itself, so this value is always 1 or more; if parameters were provided, it will be 2 or more.

char *argv[]; now that's confusing, right? This is actually a composite of a few things we've already seen. There's a ***** in there, so it's a pointer; the type is **char**, so there are characters in it, and there are square brackets, so it's an array…

This is actually an array of pointers to characters; each element of the array is a string, and each string is one of the parameters provided to the program.

[SCANF]

Just like **sscanf**, **scanf** returns an integer indicating how many values it successfully read, which you can use to check for errors. One problem is that **scanf** only removes matched values from the input buffer, so if a **scanf** fails to match anything, what the user typed will be read again on the next call to **scanf**. It really is easier to use **fgets** and **sscanf**!

It's probably easier to understand that in practice:

```c
#include <stdio.h>

int main (int argc, char *argv[])
{
  int param = 0;
  while (param < argc)
  {
    printf ("Parameter %d is %s\n", param, argv[param]);
    param++;
  }
  return 0;
}
```

[GET THE NUMBER RIGHT]

Remember that the first item in the argv array - argv[0] - is the name of the program itself, not the first parameter. The actual parameters start at argv[1].

Try running this as before, just by typing its name. Then try typing other things after the name on the command line and see what the program prints.

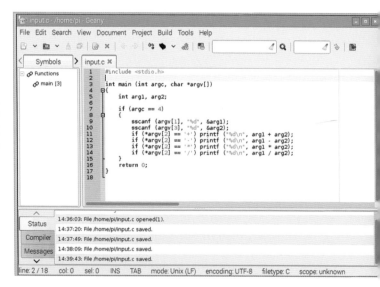

Right The argc and argv arguments to the main function can be used to access parameters typed on the command line when the program is run

Here's an example of a (very) simple calculator written using program parameters:

```
#include <stdio.h>

int main (int argc, char *argv[])
{
  int arg1, arg2;
  if (argc == 4)
  {
    sscanf (argv[1], "%d", &arg1);
    sscanf (argv[3], "%d", &arg2);
    if (*argv[2] == '+') printf ("%d\n", arg1 + arg2);
    if (*argv[2] == '-') printf ("%d\n", arg1 - arg2);
    if (*argv[2] == 'x') printf ("%d\n", arg1 * arg2);
    if (*argv[2] == '/') printf ("%d\n", arg1 / arg2);
  }
  return 0;
}
```

[CHECKING RETURN VALUES]

In Linux, the return value from a program isn't shown, but is stored and can be read from the command line. If you type **echo $?** immediately after running a program, the value the program returned will be shown. Return values are mainly useful if you're calling programs from scripts.

Note that we use ***argv[2]** to get the first character of the second parameter. This should only ever be a single character, but because each of the arguments can be a string, **argv[2]** (without the asterisk) is a pointer to a character, not the single character required for a comparison using **==**.

Make sure you separate the arguments from the operator with spaces so they're identified as separate parameters; **<progname> 2 + 2** rather than **<progname> 2+2**.

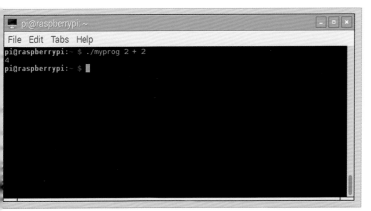

Left The calculator reads the two values and the operator from the **argv** array and prints the result

[CHAPTER TEN]
FILE INPUT
AND OUTPUT

Reading from and writing to files

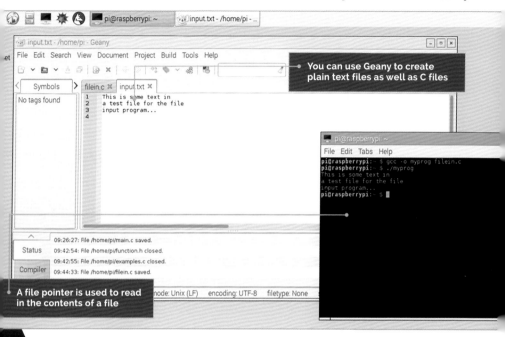

You can use Geany to create plain text files as well as C files

A file pointer is used to read in the contents of a file

In the previous chapter, we looked at how to get input from the user at the console. In this chapter, we'll look at the other common method of input and output in C: reading and writing files.

Many programs need to be able to access files on the host computer's disk; even if it's just for saving user preferences and the like, file access is a fundamental requirement for a lot of programming tasks.

In C, files are accessed by use of *file pointers*. A file pointer contains all the information required to access a file: both its name and location on the file system, and the current position within the file at which data will be read or written.

So the first thing we need to do is to get a file pointer. This is done using the C function **fopen**, which takes two arguments. The first argument is the path to the file, including its name and extension. The second argument is called the *file access mode*; this is a code which indicates whether you intend to read from the file or write to it.

Let's look at an example of reading a file. Use your text editor to create a file called **input.txt** in the **/home/pi** directory on your Pi, and type anything you like into it. Save it, and then create and run the following program:

```
#include <stdio.h>

void main (void)
{
  FILE *fp;
  int value;

  fp = fopen ("/home/pi/input.txt", "rb");
  if (fp)
  {
    while (1)
    {
      value = fgetc (fp);
      if (value == EOF) break;
      else printf ("%c", value);
    }
    fclose (fp);
  }
}
```

[ALWAYS CHECK YOUR FILE POINTER]

Never assume that **fopen** has worked - always check that the value it returns is a valid pointer (i.e. not zero). If you try to read from a zero pointer, you'll get random nonsense; if you write to a zero pointer, you'll probably crash the computer!

First, we declare a file pointer variable called **fp**, which has the type **FILE ***. We also declare an integer which we'll use to hold the characters read in from the file.

We then create the file pointer using the command **fopen** (for 'file open'). We open the file at **/home/pi/input.txt**, and we set the mode to **"rb"**, which indicates 'read binary'. This creates the file pointer and initialises it to the beginning of the file.

We then check to see if the file pointer is non-zero; if the pointer is returned as zero, the file wasn't successfully opened. (For a read, this usually indicates that the file doesn't exist.)

If the file pointer does exist, we call the function **fgetc** (for 'file get character') in a loop; each time this function is called, it reads a single byte from the file, and then advances the file pointer to the next byte in the file. When the file pointer reaches the end of the file, it returns the special value **EOF** (for 'end of file'). So we print the value returned by **fgetc** each time until it returns **EOF**.

Once we have finished reading the file, we finish access to it by calling **fclose** (for 'file close'), which frees the file pointer and allows you to reuse it to access another file.

Note that while **fgetc** reads characters, it returns an integer; this is because the code for **EOF** falls outside the valid range of a char variable (0 – 255). Unless at the end of a file, **fgetc** returns an integer value which can always be treated as a char.

Writing a file

To write to a file, we use a file pointer in exactly the same way, but we open it in a mode for writing.

```c
#include <stdio.h>

void main (void)
{
  FILE *fp;
  int value;

  fp = fopen ("/home/pi/output.txt", "wb");

  if (fp)
  {
    for (value = 48; value < 58; value++)
    {
      fputc (value, fp);
    }
    fclose (fp);
  }
}
```

[REMEMBER TO FCLOSE]

It's easy to forget to call **fclose** on your file, but it's important to do so. On some systems, when writing to the file system, the write doesn't actually complete until **fclose** is called; if your program doesn't call **fclose**, you might find that you write to files and nothing shows up in them.

In this case, we open the file **/home/pi/output.txt** with the mode **"wb"**, which indicates 'write binary'. This opens the file for writing; if this file already exists, the contents are deleted.

We then call the function **fputc** (for 'file put character') in a loop, writing the bytes 48, 49…57 to the file. (These are the character codes for the text characters for the 10 digits 0, 1…9). As before, we then close the file pointer. If you run this and then look in your home directory, you should find the file **output.txt**, containing the string **0123456789**.

Right Reading or writing a file requires a file pointer to be opened with **fopen**, and the resulting pointer is then used in all operations. Remember to close the pointer afterwards with **fclose**

Formatted output

fputc is useful for writing bytes to a file, but it's an inconvenient way of writing text to a file. For this, we can use the **fprintf** function ('file print formatted').

```c
#include <stdio.h>

void main (void)
{
  FILE *fp;

  fp = fopen ("/home/pi/output.txt", "wb");

  if (fp)
  {
    fprintf (fp, "This is some text.\n");
    fclose (fp);
  }
}
```

fprintf works in exactly the same way as **sprintf**, but the first argument is a file pointer rather than a string.

Moving around a file

Quite often, rather than overwriting a file, we just want to add to the end of it. To do this, open it with **fopen ("/home/pi/output.txt", "ab");** – **"ab"** indicates 'append binary'. If the file exists, output will then be added after the existing file contents; if the file doesn't exist, it will be created and output will start at the beginning.

Sometimes when accessing a file, we don't necessarily want to start at the beginning. The **fseek** function can be used to reposition the file pointer within the file.

```c
#include <stdio.h>

void main (void)
{
  FILE *fp;
  int value;

  fp = fopen ("/home/pi/input.txt", "rb");
  if (fp)
  {
    fseek (fp, 10, SEEK_CUR);
    while (1)
    {
      value = fgetc (fp);
      if (value == EOF) break;
      else printf ("%c", value);
    }
    fclose (fp);
  }
}
```

The line **fseek (fp, 10, SEEK_CUR)** moves the file pointer 10 bytes ahead of the current position, so this program will print all but the first ten characters in the file. The first argument to **fseek** is the file pointer; the second is the offset by which the pointer is to move. This can be positive or negative; so **fseek (fp, -5, SEEK_CUR)** moves the pointer 5 bytes back from the current position.

The third argument to **fseek** allows you to choose a position relative to the start of the file (**SEEK_SET**) or the end of the file (**SEEK_END**) rather than the current position. So **fseek (fp, 12, SEEK_SET)** positions the pointer 12 bytes ahead of the start of the file, while **fseek (fp, -17, SEEK_END)** positions it 17 bytes back from the end of the file.

enumerations, and structures

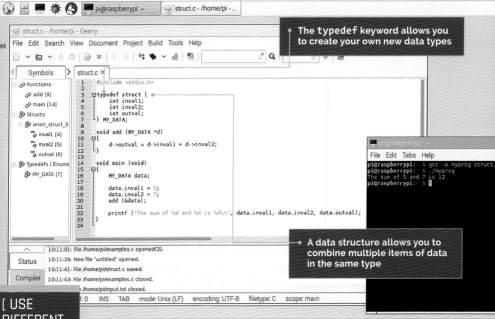

The **typedef** keyword allows you to create your own new data types

A data structure allows you to combine multiple items of data in the same type

n this chapter, we're going to look at some of the more advanced topics around the use of variables and types, including the difference between local and global variables, defining new types, and the use of enumerations and data structures.

When we've used variables in the examples in this book, we've always put them inside function definitions. These are therefore *local variables*; that is, variables which are local to those functions and have no meaning outside the function.

Global variables

C also allows *global variables*; that is, variables which are defined outside all functions. These have global *scope*, which means they can be read and written from any function within the program. Let's look at an example:

```c
#include <stdio.h>

int result;

void add (int a, int b)
{
```

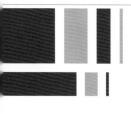

```
    result = a + b;
}

void main (void)
{
    add (3, 4);
    printf ("The result is %d\n", result);
}
```

In this example, the variable **result** is global. It can therefore be read or written within both the **add** function and the **main** function; as you can see, we write a value to it in **add** and read it back in **main**, and so we don't need to return a value from **add**.

In some ways, this looks easier than passing values about all over the place, surely? So why not just do this all the time? The answer is memory. Local variables in functions are temporarily allocated space while the function is running, and the memory is freed up as soon as the function ends. But global variables are allocated space when the program starts, and that space isn't freed until the program ends; if you allocate enough of them, you can run out of memory on some systems.

There's a better way of making a lot of data available to every function, which we will come to a bit later on…

Type definitions

In a previous chapter, we looked at the range of variable types in C: **char**, **int**, **float**, and so on. C also allows you to define your own types, with what is known as a *typedef*. A typedef is a line of the format **typedef <existing type> <new name>**, usually put at the start of a program. For example:

```
    typedef unsigned char BYTE;
```

This defines a new type called **BYTE**, which is another name for an **unsigned char**. (Note that by convention, user-defined types are usually given names in capital letters. It's not compulsory, but it does help to distinguish them from variables when reading the code.)

When we say this defines a new type, what it really does is to create an alias to an existing type. This seems a bit pointless, but it can help in two ways. First, it can make it more obvious what your code is doing if you make the type names specific to your program's data. Second, by defining specific types, you can get the compiler to warn you if you use the wrong type for a function argument or variable.

There are a couple of specific cases where typedefs are particularly useful: these are enumerated types and data structures.

Enumerated types

Often, there's a use for a variable which can only take one of a few possible values. C provides a type called **enum** for this purpose, which defines an integer with a fixed set of named values. Here's an example:

```c
#include <stdio.h>

typedef enum {
    false,
    true
} BOOLEAN;

void main (void)
{
    BOOLEAN b_var;

    b_var = false;
    if (b_var == true)
    {
        printf ("TRUE\n");
    }
    else
    {
        printf ("FALSE\n");
    }
}
```

[NUMBERED ENUMS]

When you create an enum, the compiler assigns a numeric value to each of the possible values. By default, it numbers the first in the list as 0 and counts up from there. You can override this by putting an equals sign after each named value and setting it to the value you want.

As you can see, the named values of the enumerated type are used instead of numbers for assignments and comparisons. This can make code a lot easier to understand, and is a very good way of preventing errors, as an enumerated variable can only ever be set to a valid value.

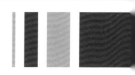

Structures

The other really useful thing you can do with a typedef is to use it to define a *data structure*. This is a collection of individual variables which are grouped together, allowing you to pass the structure between functions rather than the individual variables.

Here's an example:

```c
#include <stdio.h>

typedef struct {
  int inval1;
  int inval2;
  int outval;
} MY_DATA;

void add (MY_DATA *d)
{
  d->outval = d->inval1 + d->inval2;
}

void main (void)
{
  MY_DATA data;

  data.inval1 = 5;
  data.inval2 = 7;
  add (&data);

  printf ("The sum of %d and %d is %d\n", data.inval1,
    data.inval2, data.outval);
}
```

So here we use a typedef to create a data type called **MY_DATA**. The definition of the structure consists of the keyword **struct** with a list of variables enclosed by curly brackets; in this case, the structure consists of three integer variables.

In the **main** function, we declare an instance of the structure as a variable called **data** of type **MY_DATA**. We then access the individual

Below An instance of the MYDATA structure is used
to pass the three integers to the add function

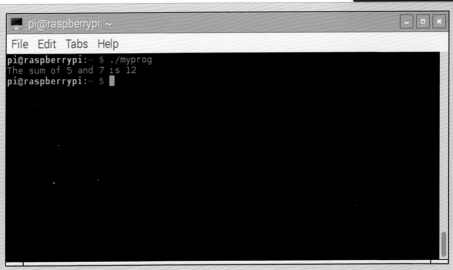

elements of the structure by giving the name of the structure
variable (**data**), a full stop (**.**), and the name of the specific element.
So the line **data.inval1 = 5** sets the value of the element **inval1**
of **data** to 5, and so on.

The function **add** takes a pointer to a **MY_DATA** structure as its
only argument; as ever, a function cannot change the values of its
arguments, but can change values pointed to by its arguments,
so we pass a pointer rather than the structure itself.

To access the elements of a structure from a pointer to it, we replace
the full stop with an arrow made up of a minus sign and a greater than
sign (**->**). So the **add** function reads the values of **inval1** and **inval2** in
the structure pointed to by **d**, and then writes the result back to **outval**
in the same structure; the **main** function then prints the result from
the structure.

Structures are very useful if you need to pass a lot of data around
between functions; they can be a lot more memory-efficient than
having large numbers of global variables, as you only need to create
the structure as and when you need it, rather than taking up memory
all the time.

[. VS ->]

When
accessing a
structure's
elements,
make sure you
use the right
symbol. A . is
used if your
variable is an
instance of the
structure itself;
a -> is used if
your variable
is a pointer to
an instance of
the structure.
Using the
wrong one will
usually give
an error from
the compiler.

CHAPTER TWELVE
HEADER FILES
AND THE
PREPROCESSOR

Splitting code up into multiple files

Every use of the symbol PI is replaced by the value in the matching #define directive

All preprocessor directives, like #define, start with a # sign

A ll the examples we've seen so far have put all the code for a program in a single C file. But once programs get big, it makes more sense to be able to split them up into separate files, grouping similar functions together. To understand how this works, we need to look in more detail at what the compiler actually does.

In all the examples so far, we've called gcc on a single source file and it has created a single executable program. This hides the fact that gcc actually does two things: first, it compiles your C source file into what's called an *object file*, and then it *links* the object file with all the library functions to create the executable. This second step is performed by a program called a *linker*; gcc actually does both jobs.

If you create a program with multiple source files, you just need to include the names of all the source files in the call to gcc. It will then create one object file for each source file, and then link all your object files together to create the executable.

There's one snag, though. If you've separated your code into separate files (usually referred to as *modules*), you'll have some files which make calls to functions in other files in order to work. These files don't find out about each other until the linker operates on them; the files are compiled individually, and the compiler will complain if you use functions in a file it doesn't know about.

We fix this using _header files_. These are files with the extension **.h** which hold the declarations of functions defined in a module, so that the compiler can be told about them when they're used by another module. We've already seen this many times; remember that line **#include <stdio.h>** at the top of the examples? That is exactly this process; it's telling the compiler that functions declared in the system header file **stdio.h** are used in this module.

Splitting code into multiple files

Let's look at an example of how this works. Create three files, two with the extension **.c** and one with the extension **.h,** as follows:

function.c

```c
int add_vals (int a, int b, int c)
{
   return a + b + c;
}
```

function.h

```c
extern int add_vals (int a, int b, int c);
```

main.c

```c
#include <stdio.h>
#include "function.h"

void main (void)
{
   printf ("The total is %d\n", add_vals (1, 2, 3));
}
```

Put all three files in the same directory and run gcc, giving it the names of both **.c** files – **gcc -o myprog main.c function.c**.

The resulting program will run the **main** function from **main.c**, which calls the **add_vals** function from **function.c**.

A few things to note. First, inside the header file we declare the

Left The add_vals function is called from the main function - the linker connects the call from main.c to the function definition in function.c

function with the word **extern** at the start of the declaration. This tells the compiler that this function is to be found externally to the file, i.e. in another C file.

Second, while we have always included **stdio.h** with its name between **<>** signs, we include **function.h** in double quotes. The **<>** signs tell the compiler to look for the file in the directory where the system's include files are stored; the **""** signs indicate that the file is local and is in the same directory as the **.c** files you're building. If you're creating your own header files, always use double quotes around the name when including them.

The preprocessor

So what does **#include** actually do? It's an instruction to the *preprocessor*, which is the first stage of compiling; it substitutes text within source files before passing them to the compiler itself. The preprocessor is controlled with what are called *directives*; these are easy to spot, as they all start with a **#** sign.

The **#include** directive instructs the preprocessor to replace the line with the file which it's including. So in our example above, the line **#include "function.h"** in the **.c** file gets replaced with the contents of the file **function.h,** meaning that what's passed to the compiler looks like:

```
#include <stdio.h>
extern int add_vals (int a, int b, int c);

void main (void)
{
  printf ("The total is %d\n", add_vals (1, 2, 3));
}
```

[MAKEFILES]

As you can imagine, if you have a project with tens or hundreds of C files, typing all their names in the call to gcc every time would be a bit tedious! Large projects are built with a tool called "make", which stores build instructions in a "Makefile". Makefiles are outside the scope of this book, but there's lots of information about them online.

#define

Another useful directive is **#define**, which can be used to define constant values. Look at this example:

```
#include <stdio.h>
#define PI 3.14159

void main (void)
{
  float rad = 3;
  float circ = rad * 2 * PI;
  float area = rad * rad * PI;
  printf ("The circumference of a circle radius %f is  %f\n",
        rad, circ);
  printf ("The area of a circle radius %f is %f\n", rad, area);
}
```

The directive **#define** is used to set the value of pi. The important thing to remember is that **PI** isn't a variable; it's text that will be substituted by the preprocessor. The **#define** line tells the preprocessor to go through the file and replace every instance of the symbol **PI** with the digits **3.14159** before passing it to the compiler. So a line which does something like **PI = 5;** will cause an error; the compiler will see the meaningless statement **3.14159 = 5;**.

Why is this useful? Why not just declare a float variable called **PI** and set it to 3.14159? A floating-point variable requires allocating memory in which to store it; using **#define** saves that memory, which is useful if memory is limited.

You can also **#define** functions:

```
#include <stdio.h>
#define ADD(a,b) (a+b)

void main (void)
{
  printf ("The sum of %d and %d is %d\n", 5, 2, ADD(5,2));
  printf ("The sum of %d and %d is %d\n", 3, 7, ADD(3,7));
}
```

Again, this does a text substitution; whenever **ADD(a,b)** appears in the code, it's replaced by **(a+b)**, with the values of **a** and **b** replaced by the arguments to **ADD**.

The preprocessor can also evaluate conditions with the **#if** directive:

```
#include <stdio.h>

void main (void)
{
#if 0
  printf ("Some code\n");
#else
  printf ("Some other code\n");
#endif
}
```

With a 0 after the **#if**, the code between the **#if** and the **#else** doesn't get called, but the code between the **#else** and the **#endif** does. If you change the value after the **#if** to a 1, the code between the **#if** and the **#else** does get called, but the code between the **#else** and the **#endif** doesn't. This is a really useful trick to temporarily remove or replace a piece of code when you're debugging.

[#DEFINES FOR TEXT]

If you use #define for text strings, they should be enclosed in double quotes, otherwise the replaced text will end at the first space. So use #define MY_TEXT "This is some text to replace." The double quotes are included in the replacement, so you can then just call printf (MY_TEXT);

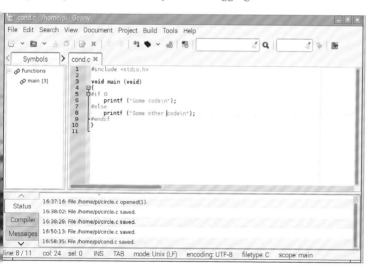

Left The most common use of #if is for temporarily removing code - just wrap it between an #if 0 and an #endif. The #else is optional, but sometimes you want to substitute the code you've removed with different code.

NEXT STEPS

This book is intended as an introduction to the C programming language for beginners. It's not a complete description of every detail of C; such a book would be at least twice the length of this one, and would cover a lot of material that even experienced programmers don't use on a regular basis.

The definitive reference on C is the book "The C Programming Language", by Kernighan and Ritchie, now in its second edition. If you've followed and understood all the material here, and want to know about the more advanced aspects of C, it's a good place to look next.

[CHAPTER THIRTEEN]
QUICK
REFERENCE

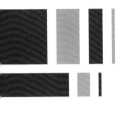

CONTROL STRUCTURES

If

```
if (<test>)
  <code executed if test is true>
```

If-else

```
if (<test>)
  <code executed if test is true>
else
  <code executed if test is false>
```

Multiple if-else

```
if (<test1>)
  <code executed if test1 is true>
else if (<test2>)
  <code executed if test1 is false and test2 is true>
else
  <code executed if test1 is false and test2 is false>
```

Switch

```
switch (<variable>)
{
  case <testval1> : <code executed if variable is testval1>
                    break;

  case <testval2> : <code executed if variable is testval2>
                    break;

  default :         <code executed if variable is neither
                        testval1 nor testval2>
                    break;
```

Switch with fall-through

```
switch (<variable>)

    case <testval1> :   <code executed if variable is testval1>

    case <testval2> :   <code executed if variable is either testval1
                            or testval2>
                    break;

    default :           <code executed if variable is neither
                            testval1 nor testval2>
                    break;
```

In all loops, the keyword **break** can be used to exit the loop and resume execution immediately after the loop.

In all loops, the keyword **continue** can be used to skip code remaining in the body of the loop and resume execution at the next iteration of the loop test.

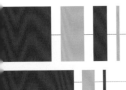

While

```
while (<test>)
  <code executed repeatedly while test is true>
```

Do-while

```
do
  <code executed once and then repeatedly while test is true>
while (<test>)
```

For

```
for (<initial condition>; <increment>; <termination conditio
  <code executed repeatedly until termination condition is tr
```

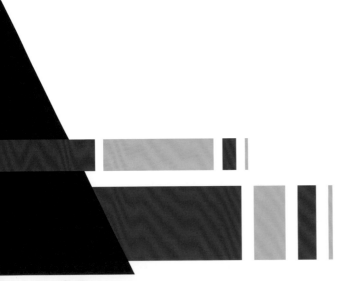

VARIABLE TYPES

Name	Description	Size (bytes)
char	Single alphanumeric character	1
signed char	Signed 8-bit integer (-128 - 127)	1
unsigned char	Unsigned 8-bit integer (0 - 255)	1
short, signed short	Signed 16-bit integer (-32768 - 32767)	2
unsigned short	Unsigned 16-bit integer (0 - 65535)	2
int, signed int	Signed 32-bit integer (-2147483648 -2147483647)	4
unsigned int	Unsigned 32-bit integer (0 - 4294967295)	4
long, signed long	Signed 32-bit integer (-2147483648 - 2147483647)	4
unsigned long	Unsigned 32-bit integer (0 - 4294967295)	4
float	Floating-point value (+/- 3.402823 x 10^{38})	4
double	Double-precision floating-point value (+/- 10^{308})	8

Depending on platform, **int** can be either a **short int** (16 bits) or a **ong int** (32 bits); on Raspbian, as per the table above, **int** is a long 32 bit) integer value.

FORMAT SPECIFIERS

Specifier	Format / type
%c	Alphanumeric character – **char**
%d	Signed decimal value – **int**
%ld	Signed decimal value – **long int**
%u	Unsigned decimal value – **int**
%lu	Unsigned decimal value – **long int**
%o	Octal value – **int**
%lo	Octal value – long **int**
%x, %X	Hexadecimal value – **int***
%lx, %lX	Hexadecimal value – **long int***
%f	Floating-point value – **float**
%e	Exponential value – **float**
%s	Text string – **char pointer**

* **%x** displays a value as hexadecimal with lower-case letters a through f; **%X** displays it with upper-case letters A through F.

The width (or minimum number of characters printed) can be set by inserting a number between the **%** and the letter; this will pad a value shorter than this with spaces at the start. To pad with spaces at the end, insert a **-** between the **%** and the number. To pad with leading zeroes, insert a **0** between the **%** and the number.

For example, to print an integer variable with the value 42, using the format specifier **"%5d"** will print 42 with three spaces before it. The format specifier **"%-5d"** will print 42 with three spaces after it. The format specifier **"%05d"** will print it as 00042.

The number of decimal places shown for a floating-point or exponential value can be set by inserting a decimal point followed by a number between the **%** and the letter; this can be combined with a width by putting the width before the decimal point.

For example, to print a floating-point variable with the value 76.54321, using the format specifier **"%.2f"** will print it as 76.54. The format specifier **"%08.2f"** will print it as 00076.54. (Note that the decimal point takes up one character of the specified width.)

OPERATORS

The operators in the table below produce a result which can be assigned to another variable, i.e. **c = a + b**, but do not affect the values of **a** or **b**.

Symbol	Function
a + b	Addition
a - b	Subtraction
a * b	Multiplication
a / b	Division
a % b	Modulo (calculate remainder)

a & b	Bitwise AND
a | b	Bitwise OR
a ^ b	Bitwise XOR
a << b	Bit shift left
a >> b	Bit shift right
~a	Bitwise 1's complement
!a	Logical NOT

The operators in the table below modify the value of **a** directly.

Symbol	Function
a++	Increment **a** by one*
a--	Decrement **a** by one*
++a	Increment **a** by one*
--aa	Decrement **a** by one*
a += b	Increment **a** by **b**
a -= b	Decrement **a** by **b**
a *= b	Multiply **a** by **b**
a /= b	Divide **a** by **b**
a %= b	**a** = remainder of **a** / **b**

a &= b	Bitwise AND **a** with **b**
a |= b	Bitwise OR **a** with **b**
a ^= b	Bitwise XOR **a** with **b**
a <<= b	Bit shift **a** left by **b**
a >>= b	Bit shift **a** right by **b**

*The difference between **a++** and **++a** is if they are used in a test, such as **if (a++)**, **a++** tests the value and then increments it, while **++a** increments the value first and then tests the incremented value.

The operators in the table below are used for comparisons in tests.

Symbol	Function
==	Is equal to
!=	Is not equal to
>	Is greater than
<	Is less than
>=	Is greater than or equal to
<=	Is less than or equal to

The MagPi Magazine

raspberrypi.org/magpi